D1518383

TIKI

OF HAWAI'I

Otau-n
Otau m

3

(above) A benevolent, whimsical tiki carved in modern times, made from coconut palm materials, watches over resort guests on a shoreline trail along the Kohala coast.

(opposite) One of several establishments to capture Waikīkī's ambiance of the mid-1900s, La Mariana Sailing Club on the Island of O'ahu boasts an eclectic décor of tiki era collectibles.

(previous page) Sketch by Louis Choris, created in the winter of 1816-1817. (*Voyage Pittoresque autour du Monde*, 1822)

TIKI
OF HAWAI'I

A HISTORY OF GODS AND DREAMS

SOPHIA V. SCHWEITZER

Mutual Publishing

At the International Market Place in Waikīkī, vendors sell exaggerated tiki carvings that celebrate the message: "Just hanging loose in Polynesia."

(opposite) A French Polynesian woman poses with a tiki, happily merging tiki's old spiritual significance with modern tourist demands.

ISBN 1-56647-749-2
Library of Congress Catalog Card Number: 2005930353

Design by Emily R. Lee

First Printing, October 2005
1 2 3 4 5 6 7 8 9

Mutual Publishing, LLC
1215 Center Street, Suite 210
Honolulu, Hawai'i 96816
Ph: 808-732-1709 / Fax: 808-734-4094
E-mail: mutual@mutualpublishing.com
www.mutualpublishing.com

Printed in Taiwan

TABLE OF CONTENTS

APPENDICES

(above) After coming ashore at Kealakekua, Captain Cook was escorted by kāhuna to Hikiau Heiau, as illustrated in this drawing by John Webber. Some think that this ceremony honored Cook as a great chief, others believe it revered him as the god Lono.

(above left) A CD cover features a modern tiki in front of the Canoe House at the Ilikai Hotel, Honolulu.

(above) A Tiki on the beach at Rangiroa, French Polynesia.

Ancient Polynesian island religions revered Tiki, in numerous aspects and under different names, as the first deity, the one who created life. For centuries, his image, carved in wood, bone, or stone, was used in prayer to summon him. Eventually, influenced by Christianity, the traditional religions collapsed. The old religion in Hawai'i would crumble in 1819. Its tiki carvings, called ki'i in the Hawaiian language, were destroyed, mostly by the Hawaiians themselves.

Meanwhile, Polynesian island life with its swaying palm trees, half-naked women, and handsome strong warriors spoke to the imagination of western explorers. For them, here was an Eden on earth. Sailors spun tall tales of a roman-

In Waikīkī, tourist shops draw attention to themselves with bizarre tiki carvings.

tic, simple, pure way of life, so different from the West. By the early 1900s, industrializing America developed a passionate longing for the South Seas as presented by a new Polynesian myth.

By the middle of the twentieth century, in faux jungle scenes and rum-laced jungle bars across America, a hang-loose South Sea ambiance exploded into a feverish cult. Americanized and commercialized, Tiki was resurrected as a symbol for the carefree life. As Hawai'i slowly succumbed to American control, its distinct cultural reality became blurred by the Polynesian fantasy. Hawai'i's statehood, in 1959, intensified tiki mania. Tiki-style mai tais, beach boys, hula girls, and ethnic jazz inebriated beatnik tourists who flocked to 1960s Waikīkī.

In the 1970s, the tiki era phased out, cooled by the priorities of a younger generation. The tiki souvenirs of the mid-1900s have become prized vintage collectibles, sweet reminders of easier times. Hawaiian culture resurfaced and regained its pride. Spiritual traditions, cultural arts, and significant sites were revitalized and restored.

Today, the most profound truth of the Hawaiian religion—the interconnectedness of all life—is vibrantly alive: It lives in islanders' respect for the land—easily sensed when you visit Hawai'i's sacred ki'i sites. It lives in Hawaiian generosity and the spirit of aloha—savored when you enter a tiki-pop-culture establishment. Hawai'i's ki'i and tiki stand firm once more as symbols of what matters in life. This book endeavors to capture the spirit of both.

Throughout the islands, contemporary Polynesian artists carve and display new tiki to meet visitor demands. In this image: The artist Mana at the International Market Place in Waikīkī.

ACKNOWLEDGMENTS

The first part of this book touches upon Hawaiian cultural and religious aspects. Grateful to be able to explore the depth of Hawaiian cultural traditions, I am indebted to the numerous Hawaiian scholars and authors who have gone before me. A special thank you to Jan Morgan at the Kohala Book Shop: Your enthusiastic guidance and active support carried me through.

The second part—tiki pop in Hawai'i—delves into a fantasy era of hang-loose fun. Seeking the reality of the 1950s and '60s, I found solid ground in Sven A. Kirsten's biblical work, The Book of Tiki, then learned the facts about Waikīkī through the generous recollections of friends who remember those times so well. Thank you all. Dawn Shibano and Joleen Soares, at the Bond Memorial Public Library, thank you for always being there for my odd research requests.

Most importantly, this work could not have been completed without a careful evaluation of the entire manuscript by one of the finest experts Hawai'i has: DeSoto Brown, thank you so much. Finally, thank you, Rick Gordon, for loving to learn about Hawai'i alongside of me.

(above) Sketch by Louis Choris, created in the winter of 1816-1817 (*Voyage Pittoresque autour du Monde*, 1822).

(next page) Moai standing at Rapa Nui (Easter Island).

TIKI OF OLD

The Hawaiian carvings of old included playful support images such as this 'ōlapa wood image. At just 9-3/4 inches tall, it possibly was one of a pair and served to hold an object with its arms.

Tiki statues in Viti Levu, the main island in Fiji.

AND THEN THERE WAS TIKI

Said to be the deified ancestor of the Polynesian people, first man and first god, the procreative power from whom all life flows, Tiki, under various names and in different languages, formed the root of Polynesian religion for many hundreds of years. Tiki appeared in creation chants and old mythologies. He was a human, yet divine; a god, with human traits. The image of all men, he became a demigod. Maori legends linked him to Tane, the life-giving god. Marquesans paired Tiki with Tangaroa, the god of the sea.

A stone tiki on the island of Bora Bora in French Polynesia.

Tiki ruled the supernatural forces that governed daily life, and manifested himself in the natural world. He gave protection or brought disaster at will. His worship was essential.

Tiki's image, carved in stone or wood, summoned the god's presence and guided ritual. Hundreds of different tiki statues evolved to hold the spirit of his myriad expressions—nature gods and ancestral forces alike. Maori women used to wear small charms around their necks, *tiki*, to protect them against barrenness. In Hawai'i, master artists created sculptures, *ki'i*, to capture the divine powers. Across Polynesia, on archipelagoes thousands of miles apart, each design was a prayer, each showed reverence for Tiki's vast, unseen spiritual world.

But no one knows how old Tiki is, or where exactly he is from.

A central temple image found in Hōnaunau in South Kona on the Big Island, made of ʻōhiʻa wood and measuring 6'5" tall.

NEW ISLANDS, NEW GODS

About 1,800 years ago, and for reasons unknown, a small group of Polynesians sailed from the southern Marquesas in hand-hewn double-hulled canoes in search of new lands. Skilled navigators, they traveled at night, guided by the stars and by patterns of winds and waves. They eventually reached Hawaiian shores.

They had brought with them seeds and plants, some chickens, dogs, and pigs, as well as memories of a culture and fragments of a religion that they had long left behind. In isolation, they adapted to their new environment. Slowly, cultural values and religious expressions changed.

The Hawaiian people saw snowcapped mountains, green-forested slopes, raging rivers, fertile valleys, lava deserts, spewing volcanoes, and fish-rich reefs. Dependent on their surroundings, aware of the interconnectedness of all life, they knew that these power-

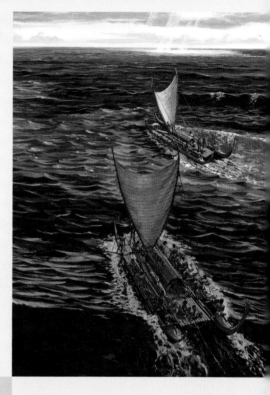

The Hawaiian people were masters with the canoe—carved, like the kiʻi, by master woodworkers. This image, painted by artist Herb Kawainui Kane, depicts what it must have been like for the first Polynesians to sail to the Islands of Hawaiʻi.

ful forces of nature could make and break their lives. They filled this diverse new home with nature spirits and protective gods—new manifestations of the ancestral deities. Spirits inhabited forests,

(above) In 1819, the French explorer Louis Claude Freycinet led an expedition to Hawai'i with the ship *Uranie*. Jacques Arago, the artist on board, created this drawing of Hawaiian life, with a woman making kapa cloth.

(left) An akua kā'ai stick image with elaborate headdress, found in a cave in Honokoa Gulch near Kawaihae on the Big Island.

trees, stones, plants, animals, lava outcroppings, rivers, waterfalls, and ponds. Religion permeated Hawaiian life.

In supreme control over nature and human affairs, the gods had to be kept at peace. Angry gods split the earth, hurled lava, and spread floods. Contented gods bestowed prosperity. It was vital that proper respect for the spirits was maintained in each daily activity. From cooking, fishing, and farming to issues of birth, marriage, and death, the Hawaiians paused to acknowledge the sacredness of life. Tools, canoes, kapa cloth, statues, medicine, taro, or gourds—everything was imbued with the supernatural.

The akua—cosmic spirits and nature deities—emanated as separate aspects of four major Hawaiian gods. From the old Polynesian world came Kāne, the life-giving creator, and his loyal companion, Kanaloa of the sea. Kū, in his many personalities, bore aggression. He became the god of chiefs and war. Lono brought agriculture, healing, games, and sports.

The 'aumakua—spirits of familiar ancestral gods—acted as protective forces for individual families.

Demigods wielded their power within the limits of a district or community.

Following their ancestral traditions, the Hawaiians carved human figures to represent and invoke their gods. These carvings were the ki'i, the tiki of old. They made the fearsome and invisible powers seem less abstract, and established contact with the spiritual realm. Akua ki'i, large wooden temple statues, were complemented by smaller stick images, staffs with carved figures and portable statues, akua kā'ai.

Temple statues in Pu'uhonua O Hōnaunau National Park on the Big Island are replica of the akua ki'i that once stood on this sacred site.

Stone images from Necker Island

STONE IMAGES OF NECKER ISLAND

The first settlers spread out over the main Hawaiian islands: Kaua'i, O'ahu, Moloka'i, Lāna'i, Kaho'olawe, Maui, and Hawai'i, known as the Big Island today. Different communities, in sporadic contact with each other, each developed their own tiki style. The settlers favored wood, available in abundance, as their carving medium of choice.

In addition, the Hawaiian people spent time in more remote places where forests were sparse. Less than two hundred miles to the northeast, on the islet of Nihoa, where rainfall is scant, at least fifteen religious structures have been found adorned with rows of upright stones. These ki'i pōhaku, stone images, must have served as gods, erected perhaps by stranded inhabitants.

Necker Island, near Nihoa, consists of vertical cliffs. Nothing grows. No one can survive for long. And yet, in the late 1800s, explorers found an ancient temple with thirteen stone basalt images. With their round faces and wide mouths, they resemble the Marquesan tiki and remain unique in Hawaiian history. We don't know who made them or what tools were used, and only a few have survived.

THE MOAI OF EASTER ISLAND AND THE MENEHUNE OF HAWAI'I

In 1947, Thor Heyerdahl, a Norwegian researcher stationed in the Marquesas, captured headlines worldwide when he sailed, on a balsa-raft made in ancient-Peruvian style, from South America to Polynesia. His journey of more than three months and 4,900 miles ended on island reefs and proved his theory that such voyages might have occurred in the distant past. This, he suggested, might indicate a connection between the Incan god Kon-Tiki and Tiki in the Marquesas, and might even tell of the origins of the Polynesian race.

It is quite certain today that the Polynesian people did not originate in South America, and, instead, trace back to Asia. Even so, legends linger of an ancient race of people, said to have inhabited the South Sea islands in a time before time. They were, so it is said, killed by a new wave of immigrants, the current Polynesian race.

Maybe they explain the mythological menehune, thought to be descendants of a tribe that inhabited the Hawaiian islands until enslavement by a subsequent Hawaiian-Polynesian race. In Hawaiian mythology, the menehune are often portrayed as hard-working little people from a low social caste.

(above) Moai guard the platform altar known as Ahu Tongariki on the south coast of Easter Island, restored in 1992.

(above left) The moai of Easter Island (Rapa Nui, Chile) were carved at the quarry of the volcano Rano Raku. While most were taken to other locations, many remained on site.

On his third expedition, after ten years as the leader in Pacific Ocean explorations, British Captain James Cook found the Hawaiian islands while commanding the ships Resolution and Discovery (as seen in the bottom image by John Webber). Events that followed would change the Hawaiian ways in irreversible ways.

THE KAPU

Over time, as the Hawaiian population grew, political and religious hierarchies became increasingly complex. By the time Captain Cook arrived in the Islands in 1778, an elaborate protocol of observances and ceremonies had evolved to maintain order and to avoid the wrath of the gods. They centered around two concepts: mana, or spiritual life force, and kapu, a complex web of prohibitions.

In strictly structured temple rituals, attended only by priests and chiefs, the ruling chief received mana, which came from the gods. Filled with mana, the chief acted on behalf of the gods and therefore held undisputed power.

The system of kapu enforced peace with the gods. It ensured that the chief's supremacy was honored. So powerful was the charge of his mana, that the chief was kapu. Commoners, too vulnerable for such energy, should not

(above) Kapu breakers risked death and might be sacrificed at the luakini. In 1819, shortly after the kapu system had been abolished, Jacques Arago, artist for the French explorer Louis Claude Freycinet, sketched this scene. (Voyage Pittoresque autour du Monde, 1822.) It is not certain, however, that clubbing took place.

(left) The largest of Hawaiian carvings encountered, this 9-foot 9-inch wooden post image was found in Kaua'i. It appears to resemble carvings that once surrounded Hale o Keawe in Hōnaunau on the Big Island.

John Webber's rendition of Hawaiian ki'i in a drawing of a heiau at Waimea on the Island of Kaua'i, titled "A Morai, in Atooi." Webber was part of Captain Cook's crew on the third expedition, which would anchor in Kealakekua Bay. He was the first to record impressions of Hawaiian culture.

come in contact with their chief. A high chief risked losing his mana when exposed to the common populace. Strict sanctions kept chiefs and subordinates apart.

Eating was surrounded by kapu: men and women did not share meals. Their food was cooked separately. Certain ritual foods—including pork and bananas—were reserved for men.

The kapu also maintained balance in the environment. To preserve natural resources and ensure continuous supplies of fish, plants, or trees, the chiefs and their delegates, the konohiki, might declare a harvesting or seasonal kapu.

The chief could use the kapu at his whim. A great fish pond or surfing beach might become a royal privilege. Royal grounds were definitely kapu. Sometimes there was a kapu on any and all sound.

Criminals and those who broke the kapu were sacrificed as offerings to the gods.

The kapu did not prevent calamity. Earthquakes and volcanic eruptions continued as before. Warfare continued. Rules were tightened in despair. The temple ki'i, which transmitted the mana of the gods, became increasingly fierce. It is said that, eventually, Hawaiian society was stifled under the momentous inflexibility of the kapu.

THE HEIAU OF KŪ AND LONO

In villages, on fishing shores, in houses, in forest clearings and other natural settings that seemed propitious, chiefs and commoners maintained heiau, shrines and temples dedicated to the deities. Only legends remain about the heiau and rituals from mythical times.

It is said in the traditions that after the arrival of the foreign priest Pā'ao, some time in the 1300s, the gods Kū and Lono came to prevail. With them developed two orders of heiau, a stricter kapu, and distinct carved images.

(above) During the harvest season, when Lono ruled, peace prevailed. In this drawing, John Webber depicts a boxing match during the makahiki festivals. The white kapa cloth on the left symbolizes Lono's reign.

(right) The staff representing Lono—the only remaining example: This 10-foot 2-inch pole could easily be carried around during makahiki rituals. At the ring below the carving, a cross piece would have held kapa, feathers, and other symbols.

Ahu'ena Heiau in Kailua-Kona on the Big Island may once have served as a luakini but was dedicated to Lono after 1810 when peace came over the islands. The temple has been reconstructed.

Thrum's *Hawaiian Annual* for 1938 lists more than five hundred heiau, scattered across the islands.

Ceremonies for the agricultural god Lono, who brought fertility and food to the land, took place in the māpele heiau. Pigs were sacrificed. Lono reigned about four months of the year, during the winter, when the star constellation of the Pleiades rose in the skies. This was the time for the makahiki festivals, for planting crops and playing sports. The ruling chief and his priests circled around the island with the Lono ki'i, an image that included kapa cloth, feathers, and birds. They collected taxes in the form of harvests and goods from the district chiefs who, themselves, carried smaller Lono images to sacred, royal meeting points. Peace prevailed.

The luakini heiau was dedicated to Kū, the warrior god. Formal and elaborate, Kū ceremonies were reserved to the ali'i and priests, performed under the most severe kapu, and demanded human sacrifice. The ruling chief, considered a direct descendant of the gods, sought his divine inspiration and confirmation of power in these most sacred heiau. The luakini were religious and political centers, where priests, the kāhuna pule, gave advice.

The luakini included platforms, terraces, stone walls, and houses for the priests, as well as an oracle tower and, often, a mausoleum for the chiefs' bones. Luakini—Thrum counted about ninety—had to be rebuilt and rededicated at every change of rulership. Bound to ceremonial protocol, only those of the highest ranks were allowed to participate in the construction. Each step required ritual.

The luakini reflected the power and wealth of the chief. Large temple ki'i guarded the entrance and stood on walls. Others, many at least twelve feet tall, stood in semicircles around the sacrificial altar where the chief put kapu breakers and defeated enemies to death. In their center stood the haku 'ōhi'a, the chief of all images.

Kū would become the personal god of Kamehameha in his effort to unite the islands under one reign. It is said that under Kamehameha's rule, some time after 1791, the classical fierce-looking Kona ki'i evolved which, about 160 years later, would become the universal symbol of the popular tiki style.

In 1791, King Kamehameha I completed Pu'ukoholā Heiau in Kawaihae on the Big Island, a massive war temple that would ensure his reign over the islands. This photo also shows an older heiau, Mailekini.

Ahu'ena Heiau as it would have been in 1816, based on a lithography by Louis Choris, titled "Temple du Roi dans la baie Tiritatea."

HAKU 'ŌHI'A, CHIEF OF ALL IMAGES

During the rededication of a luakini heiau, the central and most sacred image, the haku 'ōhi'a, was erected only after the temple had been rebuilt, when kapa decorated fences, the altar shone green with foliage, and minor images had been touched up. It was the only image that had to be made anew, and might measure up to fifteen feet tall.

The strict ceremonies that surrounded the creation of the haku 'ōhi'a started with the consecration of the adze and a slow search for the perfect 'ōhi'a tree. The soft wood of the sacred 'ōhi'a lehua was favored among all woods, its gnarly, reddish appearance a manifestation of Kāne and Kū. A human sacrifice was required where the chosen tree had been felled. A severe kapu—no disturbances, no sound—accompanied the days or weeks of carving that followed. In the temple, a second human sacrifice marked the place where the statue would stand.

Elaborate offerings accompanied final consecrations. Priests wrapped a coconut-fiber belt around the statue's belly, then cut it with a knife—a symbol of birth, the severance of the umbilical cord. Wrapped in a white kapa cloth, the image was ready to receive the god's mana, and to be the chief, haku. It is said that only this central image preserved its mana long after the end of the rituals.

(above) In 1823, Missionary William Ellis created this drawing of Hale o Keawe, the burial place of Chief Keawe (1700s) and his descendants, located within Pu'uhonua o Hōnaunau on the Big Island. When Hawai'i's temples were destroyed in 1820, Hale o Keawe and several of its wooden images were spared.

(right) Standing tall in Pu'uhonua O Hōnaunau National Park, this replica invokes the ki'i of old.

PU'UHONUA, PLACES OF REFUGE

Enforced by capital punishment, the kapu hampered daily activities. Warfare was common and bloody in Hawaiian days. And yet, across the islands, the priests oversaw specially designated sanctuaries, often on the grounds of a sacrificial luakini heiau, where even the worst murderers could find respite. Criminals, enemy warriors, kapu breakers, as well as women, children, and the elderly during times of war, could enter these pu'uhonua, high-walled places of refuge, and be safe. Not even the ruling chief himself could continue persecution. After several days of prayers and healing, those who had entered could leave, forgiven of crime.

One of the tallest ki'i in Ahu'ena Heiau, shown here as a reproduction, was crowned with a carving of the golden plover. It was associated with health and healing.

TIKI FORMS, TIKI STYLES

Only highly skilled and dedicated sculptors, the kāhuna kālai, were allowed to create the akua and 'aumakua images that captured the spirits of the ancestral gods. They were priests as much as artists. Their training and commitment started in their youth. The carving was a lengthy process filled with prayer and protocol, a spiritual and subtle task.

Tools included stone adzes and glass-sharp basalt chips chiseled high up on Mauna Kea mountain. Shark's teeth provided additional knives. Sharp-pointed shells or bones might serve as drills. Coral stone, shark skin, and rough foliage such as breadfruit leaves smoothed rough edges. Kukui nut oil gave the statue a deep, dark glow.

A three-dimensional akua kā'ai with teeth, hair, and eyes carries on its back a small figurine, which used to be one of a pair.

Hawaiian sculptors developed a vigorous style. Statues showed aggression, dynamic movement, and frightening facial features. Hands, arms, knees, and calves were stylized, three-dimensional, and distinct. Each groove, each detail, and each shape had symbolic meaning. Not a single cut was left to chance, each stroke of the knife controlled.

Portable images used in temple ceremonies and carried around, the akua kā'ai, were often wrapped in kapa cloth. They might be decorated with mother-of-pearl eyes, braids of human hair, human teeth, or teeth of sharks and dogs, and tied with streamers of cords and kapa cloth. Red feathers—a powerful sign of mana and wealth—resembled helmets and even skin. The akua

(left) Each feature of the classical, fierce, and fully-sculpted temple image was imbued with meaning in Hawaiian culture. This image stood 4 feet tall.

(right) This temple image, found at Hale o Keawe, at Puʻuhonua o Hōnaunau, shows a sculpted beard and distinct arms and hands.

kāʻai could be small stick images at the end of carrying poles, no larger than two feet tall. Or they could be free standing, several feet in height, heavy and fearsome when carried around. Some might connect with cosmic deities and nature spirits, others with family ancestors.

The fully-sculpted, regal images that Hawaiʻi is most known for today were carved from whole tree trunks. Roughly faceted, they were voluminous, sculpted to intimidate with a message of superiority, fierceness, dominance, and contempt. Used by the aliʻi to invoke mana, they kept commoners in fear. The image mimicked the pose of the wrestler, the angry chief, and the undisputed god. The enormous head with crest and large protruding jaw— startling, growling, snarling—signified the presence of stored mana. It is thought that the temple style came to its full splendor in the Kona district on the Big Island after the conquests of Kamehameha I, in the 1790s and early 1800s.

Hawai'i's master carvers expressed their artistic skills and sense of aesthetics without restraint in support figures that were not bound by religious protocol and regal meaning. Playful, acrobatic images that were friendly, fun, and helpful emerged from their knives.

VIGOROUS SCULPTURE

The ali'i owned platters, drums, poles, and vessels decorated with apparently whimsical, playful, acrobatic figures that functioned as handles, holders, or supports. Symbols of wealth and power, these image-objects show the superior artistic talent of the kāhuna kālai.

Based on sketches from the early 1800s and built near the original site in Kailua-Kona, the replica of Ahu'ena Heiau includes several carved temple images in different styles.

THE FALL OF THE GODS

Queen Ka'ahumanu, King Kamehameha's favorite wife, as portrayed by Louis Choris in the winter of 1816-1817.

After the death of a ruling chief the kapu was suspended for about two weeks, until, during coronation ceremonies, the successor asserted his power by reinstating the kapu.

But during the reign of Kamehameha I (1791–1819), Hawaiian society had dramatically changed. Traders and merchants from Europe and America brought new values and beliefs. They spoke of a god who seemed less vengeful than the Hawaiian gods and did not fear the kapu. They ate with women; they took as they pleased—without punishment. The sailors brought diseases for

On the day that he would accept the throne to become King Kamehameha II, Liholiho defied the gods that had served his ancestors.

which the Hawaiian people had no immunity. Epidemics ravaged the population, and the gods did not even spare their own images, the chiefs.

Kaʻahumanu, Kamehameha's longtime companion and favorite wife—intelligent, strong-willed, and determined—understood the changes. She was hungry for power, weary of the dominance of men, and realized that the time had come to advance herself. She decided to challenge the roots of the kapu.

(above) Ahu'ena Heiau at Kamakahonu in Kailua-Kona, where Kamehameha I spent his last days, as sketched by Louis Choris in the winter of 1816-1817.

(right) Only few Hawaiian temple images remain. This intimidating 6-foot 7-inch classical Kona-style image resides in the Peabody Museum in Salem, MA.

In 1819, when Kamehameha I died in Kailua in North Kona, sanctioned chaos replaced the kapu, as was the custom, and Liholiho, Kamehameha's young and inexperienced son from the king's marriage to his most sacred wife, Keōpūolani, prepared for the throne in Kohala. Ka'ahumanu declared herself kuhina nui, co-regent of the prince, and, with Keōpūolani's aid, she convinced Liholiho to break the kapu. When the festivities were under way and he stepped from his canoe, the prince was to go straight to the table of the women and partake of their meal.

It is said that Liholiho, just twenty two years old, was nervous but did not dare disobey. It is said that he fortified his courage with the strong liquor that the westerners brought. That November day, he staggered to the women's table and ate. The gods did not strike.

"The kapu is broken," shouted the guests.

In the weeks that followed, across the islands, the old heiau were burned and statues torn down. The destruction would continue for years. Only about thirty-five of the large temple ki'i, including three central images, would survive. In rural villages, removed from the temples, families held on to the smaller 'aumakua statues of their ancestors, but even these would eventually be destroyed under the vigilant eye of the Christian missionaries, who arrived just five months after the abolishment of the kapu.

Scattered around the world, in museums and private collections, less than two hundred statues remain. It is thought that they were mostly carved in the late 1700s.

The luakini at Pu'uhonua o Hōnaunau in South Kona, sketched by Jacques Arago in about 1819, shortly after the fall of the Hawaiian gods. (*Voyage Pittoresque autour du Monde*, 1822.)

TIKI OF AMERICA

Tropical concoctions, baskets with pineapples, lauhala mats, and a jungle-like ambiance gave weary Americans in the 1950s sultry moments of sweet respite. Aloha attire was, of course, a must.

Beautiful women in ti leaf skirts and innocent children with ukulele guitars captured America's imagination: Hawai'i became a symbol of all that was pure, simple, and good. (Photograph by George Mellen, 1937: Annie Nihipali with brothers Charles and Herbert.)

DREAMING OF A HULA MOON

On January 17, 1779, the British ships *Discovery* and *Resolution* sailed into Kealakekua Bay in South Kona on the Big Island for their second visit to Hawai'i, under the leadership of Captain

In a tragic bloodbath, after many misunderstandings, Captain Cook, four marines, and at least 25 Hawaiians died at Kealakekua Bay, February 14, 1779. (Engraving by John Webber.)

James Cook. A series of misunderstandings—at one point sailors took statues from a Lono temple to be used as fire-wood—culminated in Cook's death. Even so, Cook's crew would bring a seductive image of Hawai'i to the West.

Other explorers followed. They found palm-fringed beaches, cascading waterfalls, and generous islanders—an apparent ease of living so different from the burgeon-ing industrialization of Europe and Puritan America. Around the 1800s, embellished travel accounts started to appear, picturing Edenic islands, where natives lived in natural innocence, deities hid in carved statues, and graceful women danced with undulating hips.

When, in 1819, the Hawaiian religion collapsed and statues crumbled, when, soon after, the missionaries came and tried to suppress cultural traditions, including the hula, the early images of a simple, exotic paradise lingered in America. Hawaiʻi became a symbol of all that felt easy, romantic, carefree, good.

In 1898, the United States claimed Hawaiʻi as a Territory, and, with it, its sultry myth—now within reach as a vacation paradise. Burdened under prohibition, an economic depression, and a heavy work ethic, Americans in the 1920s and 1930s ignited their fantasies with a popular culture based loosely on Hawaiiana ways.

Tourism in Hawaiʻi gradually took off, actively pushed by the Hawaiʻi Promotion Committee and its successors. Jack London came to write about the land of leisure and lei. Later, Hollywood joined in, with *Blue Hawaii* starring Elvis Presley.

In *Blue Hawaii*, Elvis Presley and Joan Blackman would eternalize the romantic image of Hawaiʻi.

In the 1942 MSN movie *Ship Ahoy*, a flimsy plot provides the perfect excuse for tropical sensuality and dances such as the "Hawaiian War Chant," performed by Eleanor Powell in a cellophane skirt.

The dream found its center around the sunny beachfront of Waikīkī, where Hawaiian royalty and American sugar barons had also relaxed, and where the surf was good.

Oblivious to real Hawaiian culture, the visitor industry quickly Americanized Hawai'i's native arts. 'Ukulele music, outrigger canoes, and aloha shirts became a craze. By the 1930s, native girls danced hula songs in cellophane skirts. Paper lei and imitation tiki statues showed up. Statehood in 1959 propelled pop culture into a mania.

A serious, hand-carved modern tiki guards over Tiki's Grill & Bar in Waikīkī, which opened in 2002—one of several new-millennium tiki-tourist establishments in the Islands.

Stifled by the gray sobriety of their own country, striving for the Hawaiian neo-myth, hungering for a more passionate life, middle-class America adopted and adapted the image of the carved tiki, not in the least worried by its spiritual significance. In *The Book of Tiki*, an exuberant celebration of the tiki cult that evolved in America in the mid-1900s, author Sven A. Kirsten points out that Tiki, the god of creation, metamorphosed into Tiki, the god of recreation.

It did not matter that Tiki was an object of another culture's religion, and, technically, had never existed in Hawai'i at all, since the ki'i of old honored Kāne and Kū. It did not matter that Tiki in its many expressions had held rich symbolic and sensitive meaning. Tiki—snarling, ferocious, whimsical, grotesque, and stripped of any ancient context—towered as a new idol of freedom over American

In *The Book of Tiki*, Sven A. Kirsten's odyssey into the world of American tiki, carved statues take on fabled proportions and properties.

conventional life. Artists set to producing tiki statues. Manufacturers added tiki sculptures to lamps, tables, chairs, coffee cups, salt shakers, match books, necklaces—anything that could handle tiki at all.

Across America, jolly jungle establishments mushroomed—festive drinking holes resembling grass huts, adorned with kapa, lauhala, glass balls, fish nets, coconuts, pineapples, hula dolls, and shell-studded lamps. Polynesian weapons, fearsome masks and flaming tiki torches added island passion. Tiki bowling alleys. Tiki hotels. Self-respecting people owned tiki stuff and celebrated at the tiki bar. They listened to tiki music in a tiki costume, and indulged in tiki foods and drinks. The new, happy-go-lucky tiki god reigned a good thirty years, and he was huge. Ubiquitous, modern tiki statues watched.

American and commercial, tiki swept up Hawai'i in its ride.

Hawai'i's own budding visitor industry quickly adopted the American tiki dream. After the darkness of World War II, tourists fell for 'ukulele songs, flower lei, and carefree entertainment.

All hands were on deck when the ships of the Pacific Fleet rested in Pearl Harbor. Upon their arrival, hula dancers on the docks enveloped them in the tropical dream.

WORLD WAR II, JAMES MICHENER, AND ELVIS PRESLEY

The tumult of World War II, with hundreds of young soldiers stationed in tropical isles, fueled America's escapist fantasy. James Michener's fictional war stories, *Tales of the South Pacific*, published in 1947, whispered of the ultimate romance—passionate, unbridled affairs between Polynesian beauties and American soldiers in exotic settings. When, in 1959, Hawai'i joined the United States as the fiftieth state, Michener published another novel, *Hawai'i*. Tiki-cult America went crazy for its own corner of Michener's Polynesia, where hardships are merely backdrops for love.

(above) An artist's rendition of Donn Beach's tree house in the old banyan tree at the International Marketplace.

(above left) Show time at Don the Beachcomber Restaurant drew a famous crowd. Even superstar Bob Hope could be seen dancing on the floor.

DON THE BEACHCOMBER

Raised in New Orleans, a world traveler with the taste of rum and Hollywood in his veins, Donn Beach, aka Don the Beachcomber, arrived in Honolulu at the end of World War II with a Purple Heart and a vision of a polynesian village, to be built in the heart of Waikīkī.

His given name was Ernest Beaumont Gantt, but that was before he opened his first fake-palm-tree bar in Los Angeles at the end of Prohibition in 1933, before he introduced tiki culture to America. His expertise with liquor—allegedly he invented more than seventy-five tropical rum drinks—and his passion for Polynesian-themed bars had left America in a tiki trance of rum-laced drinks, Chinese-Asian foods, flower leis, and tiki torches. Don the Beachcomber outlets and their imitations rocked across the country. Donn had become an icon for the tiki life.

Naturally, Don the Beach-comber had to sample the trop-ical rum drinks he concocted with a critical tongue.

Don the Beachcomber at Waikīkī opened in 1946, and for the next twenty-plus years, it was show-time on the beach. Donn's High Talking Chief's Long House served "native" lū'au, South Seas attire required. Samoans breathed fire, knives

Don the Beachcomber came to Waikīkī with experience. He built his first Polynesian village at his home in Endocino, California, where his Hollywood harem suited him well.

flashed, jungle drums echoed, and Asian beauties showed lots of skin in the Polynesian Revue. The Beachcomber Serenaders and Martin Denny's gang performed. Tourists danced. Hula girls swayed. Elizabeth Taylor came, as did other Hollywood stars. Bedazzled tourists crowded around the bar to slurp Donn's famous pau hana drinks, the Zombie and the Missionary's Downfall, to name a couple.

After bringing a booming cultural entertainment business to Hawai'i's tourist industry, Beach himself eventually retired to an island off Tahiti, where he died in 1989, at the age of eighty-two. His nightclub would become Duke Kahanamoku's in 1960, named after and owned by Hawai'i's legendary surfer, who had returned to his Waikīkī roots.

When tiki fury fizzled on the mainland, Waikīkī would continue to lure. Faux-Polynesian lū'au and tropical drinks found in Hawai'i's new resorts their permanent place.

(opposite and above right) Don's fantasy drinks were aptly named: *The Missionary's Downfall* **anyone? A** *Zombie***?**

(above) In the 1950s, the lavish "native" lū'au feasts at Don the Beachcomber in Waikīkī were wildly popular.

The entrance to the faux jungle of Don the Beachcomber Restaurant in Waikīkī.

A gathering of tiki on display and for sale at the International Marketplace.

THE INTERNATIONAL MARKETPLACE IN WAIKĪKĪ

In the heart of Waikīkī, 2330 Kalākaua Avenue sits on royal land, known as Kaluaokau, and was formerly owned by Queen Emma, the wife of King Kamehameha IV. Upon Emma's death in 1885, her entire estate was channeled into a trust, the Queen Emma Foundation. All proceeds from any usage were destined for Honolulu's Queen's Hospital, of which she had been a principal founder. A parking lot came to Kaluaokau. Donn Beach took up office in the aerial roots of Kaluaokau's substantial banyan tree.

In 1955, Beach proposed a new use for the site—a fourteen-acre tropical "Waikīkī Village" that would blend Polynesian culture with the Polynesian dream. It was named the International Market Place. Soon, meandering pathways crisscrossed a jungle of ethnic enclaves with displays of shops, arts, crafts, and foods. The Beachcomber was, of course, at the front of it.

Over the decades, the International Market Place grew into a busy, at times seedy, always exciting, and endlessly colorful bazaar. It was the place to go for trinkets, kitsch, key rings, t-shirts, souvenirs, food, people-watching, and entertainment. Lots of tiki as well.

By the early 2000s, Waikīkī—stuck in tiki-pop—was long overdue for an overhaul. Kalākaua Avenue brightened up with greenery, walking paths, ocean views, parks, benches, and a historical trail. In 2003, the Queen Emma Foundation announced major renovations for the Market Place as well. The new version, which will include an amphitheater, a hula podium, kiosks, and eateries, is scheduled to open in 2007 or 2008. The old banyan tree will watch over the change.

The cover of Martin Denny's third album, Forbidden Island, released in 1958, remains loyal to the tiki-era vision of Hawai'i as an exotic paradise.

MARTIN DENNY'S EXOTICA

The Hawaiian tiki bar needed its own music full of dreams and longing, its own jazzy, rhythmic sounds. In 1954, Donn Beach brought Martin Denny to his Waikīkī club. Denny, forty-three years old, a classical pianist from New York and Los Angeles who had studied in South America, would perform on the Beachcomber's stage with a jazz band that he formed in 1955. Arthur Lyman and Augie Colon were part of the original team, which soon stepped up their prestige and fame at the new Hawaiian Village Hotel. Easy listening tunes received Denny's tropical feel and exotic touch through an array of ethnic musical instruments from Polynesian, Asian, and Latin worlds. Denny called his romantic, fantasy impressions "window dressing," and also "a fusion of Asian, South Pacific, Latin American, American jazz, and classical." The sound blended perfectly with tropical drinks and sultry nights. On the mainland, popular jungle-jazz composer Les Baxter was listening in.

The magic created when bird calls and nature sounds were interwoven with instrumental tones culminated in Denny's album Exotica and the song "Quiet Village," written for Denny by Baxter himself, in 1957. By 1959, Exotica topped the national charts and the tiki era had found its own musical genre—dreamy exotica.

Denny died at his home in Hawai'i Kai on March 2, 2005.

(above) Don Ho's restaurant in Waikīkī.

(above left) A natural entertainer, Don Ho reached national fame by his mid-thirties.

DON HO

From Hawaiian descent, born in the small Honolulu neighborhood of Kakaʻako in 1930, Don Ho took his local-boy talents from a small cocktail lounge in Kāneʻohe to Duke Kahanamoku's in Waikīkī in 1962 to add his resonant voice to the blossoming rage of exotica. With his backup gang, the Aliʻi, equipped with guitars, xylophones, and drums, he emerged as a suave entertainer, Hawaiʻi's own show biz man. The audience adored his sing-alongs. By 1966, Ho had two albums out. That year he released "Tiny Bubbles," the song that would propel him to national fame. When tiki exotica faded, the Don Ho show and his motto "Suck ʻem up" remained.

Victor Bergeron, aka Trader Vic, never strayed far from a tiki statue and an upscale clientele.

With a grin to fried pineapples and tropical liqueurs, Victor J. Bergeron, a young and ambitious man in Oakland, opened a modest restaurant, Hinky Dinks, in 1934. Three years

By the 1960s, Trader Vic's restaurants, which loosely imitated Polynesian architecture, dotted the American countryside. This New Guinea longhouse-style joint would come to grace Scottsdale in Arizona.

later, riding Don the Beachcomber's success, Bergeron embraced the newborn tiki cult, expanded his tropical drinks and food repertoire, and added Hawaiian themes. He changed his restaurant's name to Trader Vic's and turned his persona into a myth. The leg that he had lost to polio became the limb surrendered to a shark. He was Trader Vic, the storyteller with the tiki statue, who appealed to an upscale tiki style.

More than twenty-five Trader Vic's restaurants opened across the world, from Europe to the Middle East, often affiliated with high-end hotels. The fantasy Polynesian food served—a bizarre blend of exotic Asian ingredients that most Americans had never heard of (cilantro, wonton) and staple American favorites (cream cheese, peanut butter), satisfied all cravings for exotic, artistic, carefree fun.

In 1941, Trader Vic opened his first restaurant on Ward Avenue in Honolulu (It would later move to Waikīkī's International Market Place, a logical and appropriate location). In the 1950s, Vic did consulting for the Matson Lines, whose luxurious ships carried tourists across the Pacific to the posh hotels of Waikīkī.

By the late 1960s, Trader Vic's restaurants outnumbered Don the Beachcomber's. Tiki's greatest icons, Donn Beach and Victor Bergeron, would remain amicable rivals until Bergeron's death in 1984. Trader Vic's restaurants are still open today.

(above left) Donn Beach's rum-laced drinks, including the *Vicious Virgin*, found competition in Trader Vic's concoctions.

(above) At Trader Vic's first tavern in Oakland, the Hawaiiana theme of fishnets, glass balls, and jungle trees seduced successful-yet-unfulfilled Northern Californians.

Layered in warm saffron hues and properly adorned, the mai tai captures the essential flavors of tiki pop.

WHO INVENTED THE MAI TAI?

Tiki mania involved the serious imbibing of rum-splashed drinks disguised by fantasy names. Trader Vic's Suffering Bastard joined the Beachcomber's Vicious Virgin. Planter's Punch sided with the Test Pilot.

Legends insist that Donn Beach played around with the subtle nuances of orange and almond flavors in layered rums as early as 1933. Others claim that, in 1944, one of Trader Vic's patrons tasted Vic's latest concoction, which used similar ingredients, and exclaimed: "Mai tai roa," which, in Tahitian, was supposed to mean "Very good." Voilà: the mai tai, the greatest tiki drink of all.

Arguments among tiki beatniks heated tiki bars for a good thirty-five years. But Bergeron defended the mai tai as his creation with the last breath of his life. Bergeron also introduced the mai tai to Hawai'i's Matson Line hotels, the Royal Hawaiian and the Moana (now the Sheraton Moana Surfrider) in Waikīkī, in 1953.

(above) Smiling Polynesian beauties in jungle settings were the prop of Waikīkī's 1950s visitor industry.

(above left) Built in 1956, The Waikikian Hotel closed its doors in 1996. The tiki-style architecture unappreciated, its last remnants were demolished in 2005 to make room for expansions at the Hilton Hawaiian Village next door.

WAIKĪKĪ TIKI IN THE LATE 1950S AND EARLY 1960S

After Don the Beachcomber, other American tiki bars naturally found their way to Hawai'i. In the late 1950s came Christian's Hut. Its origins traced back to Newport Beach, where, in 1935, the film crew for *Mutiny on the Bounty* had hung out before and after trips to Catalina Island for location shooting. The spot was named Christian's Hut after the lead character, Fletcher Christian.

An industrial magnate and international builder of highways, bridges, even ships, Henry John Kaiser had visited Hawai'i as early as 1930. He did not have small tiki bars in mind when he set up shop on O'ahu but rather large development. In 1955, the owner of Kaiser Aluminum Corporation surfed the tiki wave with the start of construction of a twenty-two-acre resort, the Hawaiian Village Hotel—today the Hilton Hawaiian Village. The Shell Bar set a lively stage. Martin Denny signed on. The resort's geodesic auditorium, the Kaiser Aluminum Dome, would serve as the recording stu-

(above right) Author H. Allen Smith added plenty of tiki-style humor to *Waikīkī Beachnik*, his account of travels in Hawai'i, first published in 1956.

(above) Brimming with sensuality, King Vidor's dramatic movie *Bird of Paradise* (1932) fueled the tiki cult with stars Dolores Del Rio and Joel McCrea, together on a South Sea Isle.

dio of celebrated musicians, including Arthur Lyman. Americans gained access to Hawai'i's exotic sounds en masse.

In the Sheraton-Waikīkī Hotel in the early 1970s, Stephen Crane installed his opulent Kon-Tiki restaurant. Crane, who allegedly allowed expensive hookers in his bars to draw expensive crowds, placed fierce-looking tiki icons on anything from matchbooks to salt and pepper shakers. Some of Kon-Tiki's tikis would eventually find their way to La Mariana Sailing Club, where they can still be found today.

La Mariana Sailing Club in Honolulu has incorporated Waikīkī's tiki-era paraphernalia and whispers of the 1950s when hula maidens drew in crowds.

Duke Kahanamoku leads the Waikīkī beach boys while posing in front of the pier of the old Moana Hotel, circa 1920.

SURFERS AND BEACH BOYS

In the early 1900s, when Waikīkī first emerged as a tourist spot, Hawai'i's greatest surfers, headed by Duke Kahanamoku, formed "Hui Nalu," Club of the Waves, and started teaching curious haole how to surf on a board—Hawai'i's sacred and beloved sport. The sun-bronzed Hawaiian men of the early 1900s became known as the Waikīkī beach boys. They were the alaka'i nalu, the leaders of the wave. The ocean was their home.

Their presence and lessons brought euphoria. They stood for a lifestyle that would blend perfectly with the tiki cult. By the 1960s, tiki's cool, hang-loose island lifestyle had to include the perfect wave. You had to swim and surf like Duke. Surfers surrounded themselves with tiki amulets, their sport a religion, a spiritual high.

One by one, the original beach boys have died. The tiki era has vanished. But Hawai'i is raising a new generation of beach boys, whose hearts and souls are with their source, as before.

The grotesque, extravagant tiki from the tiki pop era would not survive trends and sensitivities in the late 1960s. Contemporary artists, however, take their tools to unconventional materials to create friendly tiki sculptures that give both old and new traditions dignity. This coconut palm tiki looks over a shoreline trail on the Kohala coast.

TIKI CULTURE COLLAPSES

HONOLULU   CHRISTIANS HUT   HAWAII

In the early 1960s, tiki culture climaxed with extravagant grandeur. Far removed from earlier, more innocent tiki symbols, such as glass balls collected from the beach, tikis in all shapes and sizes, even portraying cannibals, had become cartoons. Not a hint of cultural sensitivity was left.

(above) Christian's Hut, one of the many American tiki bars to cross the waters to Waikīkī, would be one of the first to shutter down with the vanishing of the Polynesian dream.

A new generation was coming of age. The Beatles replaced Exotica. Rich tiki foods and sweet tiki libations lost allure. In

Vietnam, the war raged on. In Hawai'i, Hawaiian artists claimed a new cultural awareness. Reality dismantled the dream. The tiki cult became an embarrassment.

During the 1970s, tiki bars closed. Thousands of tiki paraphernalia were destroyed. By the 1980s, the tiki era was a memory. In a few attics, garages, and thrift stores, fierce-faced swizzle sticks, mugs, vases, lamps, matchbooks, salt and pepper shakers, decorative statues, bookends, menu covers, and plastic lei gathered dust.

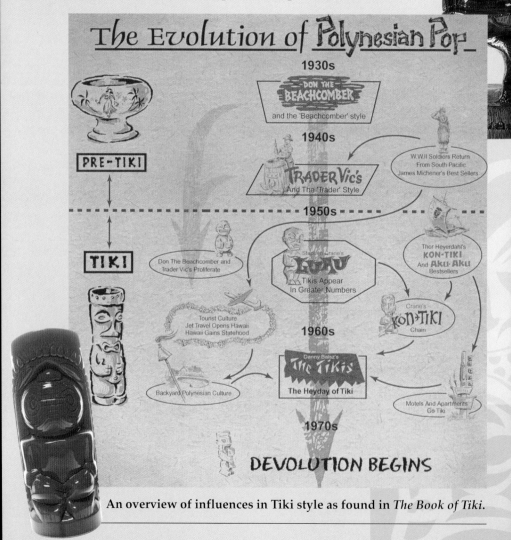

The Evolution of Polynesian Pop

1930s

DON THE BEACHCOMBER

and the 'Beachcomber' style

1940s

PRE-TIKI

TRADER Vic's
And The 'Trader' Style

W.W.II Soldiers Return
From South Pacific
James Michener's Best Sellers

1950s

TIKI

Don The Beachcomber and
Trader Vic's Proliferate

Stephen Crane's
LUAU
Tikis Appear
In Greater Numbers

Thor Heyerdahl's
KON-TIKI
And AKU-AKU
Bestsellers

Tourist Culture
Jet Travel Opens Hawaii
Hawaii Gains Statehood

Crane's
KON-TIKI
Chain

1960s

Danny Balsz's
The Tikis
The Heyday of Tiki

Backyard Polynesian Culture

Motels And Apartments
Go Tiki

1970s

DEVOLUTION BEGINS

An overview of influences in Tiki style as found in *The Book of Tiki*.

TIKI OF TODAY

Replica of ancient kiʻi at Puʻuhonua o Hōnaunau National Park watch over a sunset at the sacred site.

Anthony Pratt (left), a carver and graduate of Kamehameha School, is one of many Hawaiian artists who have kept their culture alive. Here, he presents a copy of a temple image, placed at the entrance to Bishop Museum in 1960. His craftsmanship is a testament to the early beginnings of the Hawaiian Renaissance.

SOMETHING TIKI FOR EVERYONE—
THE HAWAIIAN RENAISSANCE

During a visit of the voyaging canoe *Hōkūle'a*, after its journey to Tahiti, dancers in Hilo perform ancient hula to celebrate the revival of cultural traditions.

The buoyant tiki pop scene in Waikīkī in the mid-1900s celebrated prosperity in America. The world was recovering from the war. Hawai'i had entered the USA. Toast with a mai tai and catch a wave.

The native Hawaiians, however, had been forced to surrender their land and their culture. They stood helpless while their traditional practices became fodder for the tourist industry. The sacred ki'i and hula dance that once connected the Hawaiians to nature and spirit had been reduced to glittering imitations amid resort developments.

But under the façade, Hawaiian culture had remained vibrantly alive. When the tiki pop cult phased out, the ancient Hawaiian knowledge surged forward in what would become known as the Hawaiian Renaissance. Loyal to native wisdom, remembering the traditions of old, Hawaiian musicians recorded new songs, writers wrote, and hula dancers danced. The first double-hulled voyaging canoe to be built since the last Polynesian immigrations, the Hōkūle'a, sailed to Tahiti in 1976. With new pride, the Hawaiian people set to preserving ancient traditions and ancient sites. Although most ki'i of old were permanently destroyed starting in 1819, today some restored heiau show replicas, while museums display what could be rescued of the sculpted arts.

In 1976, when the United States celebrated the bicentennial of the Declaration of Independence, the Hawaiian canoe *Hōkūle'a* sailed to Tahiti—a voyage that once spurred Hawaiian culture, just like the voyage of the Mayflower spurred the formation of the USA.

SOMETHING TIKI FOR EVERYONE— THE TIKI POP RESURGENCE

Tiki mania of the 1950s and '60s had been culturally insensitive. And yet, it symbolized a way of life that was sweet and slow, with a carpe diem attitude increasingly foreign to modern America. Nostalgia lingers until the old truths must return. Tiki once again provides a gentle reminder of what can be, a moment of escape.

Since the year 2000, at least four books have been published brimming with photographs of tiki art—Orchids of Hawai'i mugs made in Japan, Trader Vic's salt and pepper shakers, Kon-Tiki swizzle sticks, Don the Beachcomber fans, menus, vases, candles, bar stools, ki'i carvings that draw attention to an artist's pad. Renowned American food magazines are featuring once more the nostal-

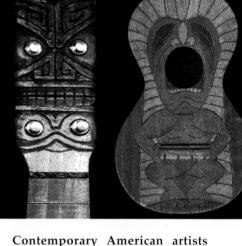

Contemporary American artists are interpreting tiki with a twist that has little to do with authenticity or with the 1950s but that is decidedly fun. Among them, Tiki King! from Santa Cruz is known for his "Tikilele," hand carved ukulele, such as this one in mahogany. Designer Paul Nielsen founded his company Munktiki, also in California, to bring to the market tiki ceramics such as this "Gold Tiki."

gic flavors of faux-Polynesian foods. Cleaned up, free of dust and mildew, vintage tiki, worthless just a decade ago, demand large sums on collectors' sites. Tiki traffic on eBay is heavy.

In Hawai'i, resorts have brought the beach boys back. Restaurants are experimenting with a beachcomber ambiance, walls dripping with oceanic memorabilia. Polynesian shows and lū'au feasts swing with modern renditions of exotica. Antique stores proudly put their tiki on display.

A replica of a ki'i at Ahu'ena Heiau in Kailua-Kona.

WHERE TO FIND KI'I OR HEIAU AND LEARN MORE ABOUT ANCIENT HAWAIIAN RELIGION

Visitors are welcome to visit the heiau listed but are asked to respect their sacredness.

THE BIG ISLAND

(above) Mo'okini Heiau.

(lower right) The only Lono staff image to have survived.

Ahu'ena Heiau 75-5660 Palani Road, Kailua-Kona, 96740 • Located on the grounds of the King Kamehameha's Kona Beach Hotel in downtown Kailua-Kona, this heiau is the replica of a temple that, in its earliest days, may have been a luakini. The ki'i, all destroyed, would have belonged to the typical Kona-style, fierce-looking tiki that developed in the last few decades before the abolishment of the kapu in 1819. Rededicated to Lono when peace came over the islands, Ahu'ena became Kamehameha's personal heiau in 1812. The king lived here until his death in 1819. The structures deteriorated rapidly in the mid-1800s, when Kamehameha's descendants moved to Hulihe'e Palace a few yards south. Later construction in the 1900s erased nearly all traces of the ancient site.

Mo'okini Heiau Turn off Highway 270 at 'Upolu Airport near Hāwī; from airport, about 1.5 miles to southwest; four-wheel drive required • On the plains of leeward Kohala, ancient Mo'okini, which may trace its origins to the fifth century, was reconstructed by the priest Pā'ao in the early 1300s to become his supreme luakini under a tighter rule of the kapu. It is said that this center of religious and political power was built in one night, with 15,000 to 18,000 men passing stones from hand to hand all the way from Pololū twelve miles north. Within the temple walls, at places six feet high and twenty feet tall, hundreds of sacrifices are said to have taken place to placate the war god Kū. The oracle tower provided splendid views of the coastline, where potential enemy fleets might be preparing for attack. Stone platforms and parts of walls remain.

Waha'ula Heiau—as it was before 1997.

WAHA'ULA HEIAU

Little is known about the ancestry of Pā'ao, the priest. The traditions say that before ascending to power in the district of Kohala, Pā'ao resided in Puna and built Waha'ula as the islands' first luakini. Said to have been one of the bloodiest places in the islands, its ki'i the last to topple after the collapse of the Hawaiian gods, Waha'ula long withstood the power of Kīlauea Volcano—lava flows destroyed a nearby National Parks visitor center—but circled around the heiau—until, in 1997, molten lava swallowed it.

Replica of classical Kona-style temple images at Pu'uhonua O Hōnaunau National Historical Park.

Pu'uhonua o Hōnaunau Route 160 off Highway. 11 toward ocean; 808-328-2326; http://www.nps.gov/puho • A National Historical Park since 1961, Pu'uhonua o Hōnaunau in South Kona, commonly known as Place of Refuge, was one of the few temples not destroyed after the abolishment of the kapu and is one of the best surviving tributes to Hawaiian religious history. Temple platforms, royal fishponds, and coastal village sites remain. Several of its classic Kona statues were saved and have found their way to museums.

In an enclosure secluded by a one thousand-foot-long wall that measured ten feet high and seventeen feet thick, possibly built in the 1500s, kapu breakers, the elderly, women and children, as well as enemy soldiers once found safety from persecution and in times of war. The heiau complex was the largest among ten pu'uhonua on the Big Island and included at least

one sacrificial luakini. Ki'i protected entrances, including the canoe landing reserved for royalty.

In the 1700s, Chief Keawe rededicated the site as his sacred home and built a house that after his death would become the mausoleum of numerous chiefs. Their bones and mana were fiercely guarded by the feathered ki'i of the gods.

The Hale o Keawe temple and several thatched structures have been recreated to capture the truths of old. Using authentic 'ōhi'a wood, a gifted Marquesan sculptor has also reproduced some of the fearsome ki'i—such as they were portrayed in early travel sketches.

Pu'ukoholā Heiau 62-3601 Kawaihae Road, Kawaihae, 96743; 808-882-7218; http://www.nps.gov/puhe • On the bluff of a hill in arid Kawaihae with strategic views of the Kona Coast, below the old heiau known as Mailekini, Kamehameha I completed his personal and massive luakini in the summer of 1791. This, an oracle had said, would give him supremacy over the islands. Thousands of laborers worked on the terraced temple of Pu'ukoholā (Eye of the Whale), which measured 224 by 100 feet with walls 20 feet thick and 20 feet high. The ground was said to tremble as chiefs from all over the island attended to the task.

At the time of the temple's final consecration, Kamehameha summoned his last remaining opponent on the island, his cousin Keōua from Ka'ū. Aware of inevitable defeat, Keōua was killed by warriors even before setting foot on Kawaihae's shore, and was offered on the altar of Kamehameha's war god Kū.

Hawai'i Island (the Big Island) thus unified, Kamehameha set out to conquer the other islands. His task was complete by 1810.

Kamehameha I would be the last ruler to honor the ki'i and the system of kapu—both served his power well. Pu'ukoholā Heiau became a National Historic Site in 1972. Entrance to the inner temple is prohibited.

Lyman Museum 276 Haili Street, Hilo, 96720; 808-935-5021; http://www.lymanmuseum.org • Although Lyman museum in

The Lyman Mission House and adjacent Museum in Hilo.

downtown Hilo has just one small, portable ki'i on display, other rare artifacts and details of ancient history abound in its exhibit halls. The home next door dates back to 1839, built by missionaries David and Sarah Lyman with 'ōhi'a and koa wood. During their mission, 'aumakua statues on home altars were often found—and quickly burned.

O'AHU

Kāne'ākī Heiau Farrington Highway, turn inland at Mākaha Valley Road, about one mile; Call 808-695-8174 before visiting • Restored in 1969 and 1970 with pili grass and 'ōhi'a wood to include prayer towers, ritual hale, an altar, and ki'i, Kāne'ākī once was a temple of peace, dedicated to Lono, the agricultural god. It may also have been a pu'uhonua. King Kamehameha I rededicated the temple to his war god Kū. The temple lies on the west side of O'ahu, in remote Mākaha Valley, on private property.

Pu'u o Mahuka Heiau Pūpūkea Road off Kamehameha Highway, between Pūpūkea and Waimea Bay Beach Park • With awe-inspiring views of the North Shore, on a bluff above Waimea Bay, Pu'u o

Mahuka (Hill of Escape) was once O'ahu's most significant political and religious center and its largest heiau. A luakini, the three-terraced temple also was a place of healing, where chiefesses came to give birth. On the National Register of Historic Places, its hundreds of feet of stone walls said to have been built by the legendary menehune, it has been partially restored.

Bernice Pauahi Bishop Museum in Honolulu.

Bishop Museum 1525 Bernice Street, Honolulu; 808-847-3511; http://www.bishopmuseum.org/ • No doubt, the largest and most impressive collection of pre-western-contact ki'i has found a home at the Bernice Pauahi Bishop Museum, which Charles R. Bishop created in 1889 as a memorial to his wife, and which has grown into the state's foremost museum for Hawai'i's natural and cultural history. The tiki collection includes large, sculpted temple images as well as kapa-wrapped portable statues and ancestor symbols. Displays and demonstrations provide insights into all aspects of ancient Hawaiian religion and culture.

MAUI
Hale o Pi'ilani Heiau Kahanu Gardens: On Hāna Highway, mile marker 31, National Tropical Botanical Garden Historical Site sign; 808-248-8912; www.ntbg.org/gardens/kahanu.html • Built for

Chief Pi'ilani, who reigned from about 1580 to 1600 AD, and is said to have brought Maui's chiefdoms under one rule, this major stone platform temple complex is the largest in Hawai'i, covering almost four acres. Walls once measured up to fifty feet tall. Although its ki'i have long been destroyed, its tropical setting and inherent sacredness offer a sense of the gods of old. The heiau, which was freed from overgrowth in the 1970s, is part of a 123-acre ethnobotanic garden, Kahanu, known for its numerous breadfruit cultivars.

Haleki'i-Pihana Heiau End of Hea Place, off Kūhiō Place off Waiehu Beach Road, look for warrior sign • Various legends speak of the building of Wailuku's great center of political and religious power, Pihana. It is said that Kamehameha I, after the bloody battle at 'Īao Valley in 1790, sacrificed a high chiefess here to rededicate the temple as the luakini for his war god Kū. Pihana, which once measured three hundred by one hundred feet, has been restored. Possibly built by Kiha a Pi'ilani in the early 1600s, three hundred feet to the northeast of Pihana, Haleki'i (House of Images) is thought to have been a chiefly compound built on an older heiau. Numerous ki'i would have guarded the stone platforms, terraces, thatched hale, and family temples dedicated to ancestral gods.

Bailey House Museum 2375A Main Street, Wailuku; 808-244-3326; http://www.mauimuseum.org • In the Hawaiian Room, in the original home of missionaries Edward and Caroline Bailey, the

THE GUARD OF KA'UIKI

After Pi'ilani's death, the throne went to his elder son. But on Hawai'i Island (The Big Island), the powerful chief 'Umi a Līloa had married Pi'ilani's daughter. He wanted Maui to be ruled by his brother-in-law Kiha a Pi'ilani, the younger son. Sometime between 1600 and 1620, 'Umi attacked Hāna's fortress, south of the Hale o Pi'ilani, on the summit of Ka'uiki, where a ferocious ki'i protected Maui against invaders from the sea. When 'Umi learned that the guard was "just" a statue, he and his army tricked the defenders and quickly won.

The Bailey House Museum in Wailuku on Maui.

Maui Historical Society has gathered numerous Hawaiian artifacts that trace the story of Hawaiian religion and culture before the overthrow of the gods.

KAUA'I

Wailua Complex of Heiau Wailua River State Park; 1.6 miles up Kuamo'o Road (580), just before 'Ōpaeka'a Falls; http://www.hawaii.gov/dlnr/dsp/kauai.html • Designated a National Historic Landmark in 1962, the sacred powerful Wailua temple site once included seven heiau. At the mouth of Wailua River, stones hint at what were the eleven-foot wide and six-foot high walls of Hikinaakalā, site of the rising sun. Possibly first built in the 1300s, Hikinaakalā was part of a pu'uhonua, Hauola, and is surrounded by river-boulder petroglyphs. It is said that a row of carved ki'i once stood on the edge of the river so they could be cleansed by its flow.

The largest remaining heiau on Kaua'i was named for the snow goddess of Mauna Kea, Poli'ahu, who, wrapped in her mantles of snow, poured life-giving water into the rivers. On a bluff above Wailua River, Poli'ahu may first have been built as early as the 1300s and is thought to have been a luakini. Legends give the menehune credit for its enormous masonry. Rock walls and foundations remain.

Kaua'i Museum 4428 Rice Street, Līhu'e, 96766; 808-245-6931; http://www.kauaimuseum.org • This small museum features a collection of Hawaiian artifacts.

MOLOKA'I

'Ili'ili'ōpae Heiau The heiau is on private property; access may be restricted. Fifteen miles east of Kaunakakai, off Route. 450, on the Wailau Trail • Possibly first erected in the 1300s, 'Ili'ili'ōpae belonged to the islands' most powerful luakini, said to have been under the spell of sorcerer gods. Measuring close to thirty thousand square feet, it was enclosed by walls up to twenty-two feet high, from which ki'i stared out over the Pailolo Channel to protect Moloka'i's chiefs. It is said that for its construction, water-worn pebbles ('ili'ili) were handed from man to man from a tributary stream in Wailau Valley several miles away. According to the legends, menehune were hired to build 'Ili'ili'ōpae Heiau. The menehune demanded whole seafoods as their pay. Expecting fish, they received tiny mountain shrimp ('ōpae) instead. Hence the name of the heiau.

The Albert Spencer Wilcox building of the Kaua'i Museum in Līhu'e was dedicated in 1924 as a library. It became a museum in 1970.

A tiki carving crowns a stair railing at the International Market Place in Waikīkī.

SHOPPING FOR VINTAGE TIKI, TIKI COLLECTIBLES, AND ALL THINGS TIKI POP

Stores and restaurants come and go in the Islands. The following addresses were current at the time of publication. They are, however, just a starting point.

THE BIG ISLAND

Mauna Kea Galleries 65-1298 Kawaihae Road, Kamuela, 96743; 808-887-2244; www.maunakeagalleries.com • A must-stop for the serious collector of vintage Hawaiiana and Polynesian art, Mauna Kea Galleries also hosts special vintage exhibits. Search here for posters, hula dolls and tiki-era figurines, hula lamps, photos, Hawaiian sheet music and tiki-era books.

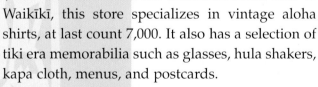

Kimo's Collection 45-3611 Māmane Street, Honoka'a, 96727; 808-963-6123 • Among an eclectic collection of wooden carvings, in an old family building in Honoka'a, lots of tiki in all shapes and sizes peek from dusty shelves.

O'AHU

Bailey's Antiques & Aloha Shirts 517 Kapahulu Avenue, Honolulu, 96815; 808-734-7628 • On the Diamond Head side of Waikīkī, this store specializes in vintage aloha shirts, at last count 7,000. It also has a selection of tiki era memorabilia such as glasses, hula shakers, kapa cloth, menus, and postcards.

Hilo Hattie For store locations or to visit the main store and manufacturing facility: 700 N. Nimitz Highway, Honolulu, 96817; free shuttle service

In 1935, the radio show "Hawaii Calls" began broadcasting from the Moana Hotel in Waikīkī. Hilo Hattie—wearing her hat—rose to international fame after joining the cast.

from selected hotels; 888-526-0299 or 808-535-6500; www.hilohattie.com • Named after the stage name for Clarissa Haili—one of the islands' popular tiki era entertainers—Hilo Hattie first opened in 1963, with a sportswear store on the island of Kaua'i. A manufacturing center in downtown Honolulu followed in 1965. The line quickly evolved into the largest one-stop retail source for souvenirs and aloha products in the state, and counts seven locations in the islands.

International Market Place 2330 Kalākaua Avenue, Honolulu, 96815; 808-971-2080; www.internationalmarketplacewaikiki.com • Scheduled to be closed for renovations, to reopen in 2007 or 2008, this was once the heart of the tiki era, right in Waikīkī, complete with cultural avenues, performances, and little shops that sold souvenirs linked to the '50s and '60s. A Polynesian local artist was often present to carve wooden tiki on the spot. At press time, details of the International Market Place's new look were still under discussion.

Ali'i Antiques of Kailua 21 Maluniu Avenue, Kailua, 96734; 808-261-1705 • With an eclectic and large selection of Hawaiiana, this windward store (across from the police station and library in Kailua) is home to lots of tiki mugs, bowls, and souvenirs.

Hale'iwa In the '60s, this little surfer's town on the North Shore of O'ahu became the favorite gathering spot for young Americans searching for a relaxed and peaceful alternative to commerce and war. The main drag sports little souvenir shops, Hawaiiana galleries, and old general stores. Polynesian tiki artists are often present to carve their work on the street.

Don Ho's Island Grill Aloha Tower Market Place, Honolulu, 96813; 808-528-0807 • Not one to be shy, Don Ho opened his eponymous grill in December 1998 at a prime waterfront location in downtown Honolulu to celebrate his trademark "suck 'em up"

Don Ho's Island Grill.

La Mariana Sailing Club.

atmosphere. Old posters, photographs, surf boards, and other nostalgic mementos adorn the place. Live Hawaiian entertainment adds spice to casual island food.

La Mariana Sailing Club 50 Sand Island Access Road, Honolulu, 96819; 808-848-2800 • A hideaway on the edge of the ocean since the mid-1950s, this little restaurant boasts Trader Vic's lamps, Don the Beachcomber's tables, Sheraton's Kon-Tiki tikis, glass balls, and an old piano, quietly capturing the nostalgia of tiki Waikīkī. When the tiki era phased out, owner Annette Nahinu simply collected whatever she could, wanting to preserve the Hawai'i she loved. A perfect place for a tropical drink and sashimi fresh from the sea.

Tiki's Grill & Bar Aston Waikīkī Beach Hotel, 2570 Kalākaua Avenue, Honolulu, 96815; 808-923-8454; http://www.tik-isgrill.com • To celebrate a tiki-era resurgence, Tiki's opened

Tiki's Grill & Bar.

in October 2002 under the watchful eye of large, concerned, hand-carved wooden tiki and with the nostalgic ambiance of a 1950s South Pacific decor. Rest assured that its menu features contemporary creations with local ingredients and fresh fish.

Tiki Shows 2300 Kalākaua Avenue, Honolulu, 96815; 808-922-4646; dinner–show package • Almost all luxury resorts in the islands host elaborate weekly lū'au feasts, which include Polynesian-style entertainment reminiscent of the 1950s and 1960s. Large shopping centers also stage tiki-style entertainment shows.

Don Ho performs at the Waikīkī Beachcomber Hotel each Sunday, Tuesday, and Thursday.

Polynesian Cultural Center 55-370 Kamehameha Highway, Lā'ie, 96762; 800-367-7060; on O'ahu, 808-293-3333; www.polynesia.com • Dedicated to the perpetuation and portrayal of the cultures, arts, and crafts of the Polynesian islands, this elaborate visitor attraction features a variety of tiki carvings, even replicas of Easter Island's stone moai. Hawaiian ki'i images guard the entrance. Recreated Polynesian villages lie scattered around the forty-two-

acre property. Lectures and demonstrations—including fire dancing, tribal tattooing, and, of course, tiki carving—delve deeply into
early Polynesian practices. Founded in 1963, the Polynesian
Cultural Center gained enormous popularity at the tail end of the
tiki pop era. It also hosts craft shops, lū'au, and shows.

MAUI

Finders Keepers 400 Hāna Highway, Kahului, 96732; 808-871-7000
• This store specializes in furniture accentuated by vintage souvenirs such as hula lamps and hula dolls that date back to dreamy
tiki days.

Pā'ia Trading Company 106 Hāna Highway, Pā'ia, 96779; 808-579-
9472 • On the north shore of Maui, the Trading Company blends
perfectly with this town's little boutiques and galleries—a throw-
back to the 1970s. Browse for Hawaiiana—tikis possibly among
them—in a collection that never stays the same.

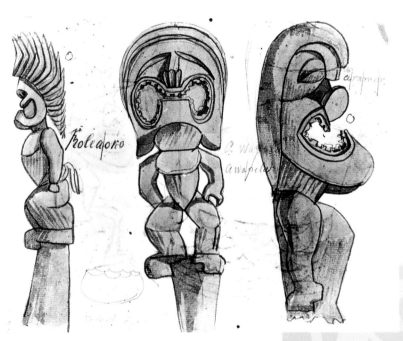

**Three authentic Hawaiian carved images, as sketched by Ukrainian artist
Louis Choris in 1816. (*Voyage Pittoresque autour du Monde*, 1822)**

The tiki of old have taken on new meaning throughout Polynesia: At the Hideaway Resort on Viti Levu in Fiji, benevolent stone statues welcome guests.

GLOSSARY

akua	cosmic deity, spirit
ali'i	chief or chiefess, ruler, king
'aumakua	family or personal god, deified ancestor
hale	house, dwelling
heiau	religious place, shrine, temple
kā'ai	sash, sennit casket; protective cloth wrapped around an object
kahuna	priest; expert in any profession
kahuna kālai	carving expert
Kanaloa (Tangaroa)	major god, companion of Kāne
Kāne (Tane)	leader of the four major Hawaiian gods
kapa	bark cloth traditionally made from paper mulberry or māmaki
kapu	prohibition, sacredness; prohibited or sacred
ki'i	image, statue
konohiki	headman overseeing a land, working for a higher chief
Kū	major god, associated with war
lauhala	pandanus leaf as used in plaiting
Lono	major god, associated with agriculture and peace
luakini	large sacrificial heiau
lū'au	feast with traditional Hawaiian foods
makahiki	period from about mid-October to January during which Lono, the agricultural god, replaced Kū, the war god, marking a time dedicated to farming and peace
mana	divine or spiritual power, life force
menehune	Hawai'i's earliest, legendary settlers
moai	Easter Island images
'ōhi'a	native tree considered sacred
pau hana	after work
pōhaku	stone
pu'uhonua	place of refuge
tiki	generic word for all wooden images associated with Polynesia

BIBLIOGRAPHY

Buck, Peter H. *Arts and crafts of Hawaii.* Honolulu: Bishop Museum Press, 1957.

Carter, Duke. *Tiki Quest: Collecting the Exotic Past.* Chicago, IL: Pegboard Press, 2003.

Cox, Halley J., and William H. Davenport. *Hawaiian Sculpture.* Honolulu: University of Hawai'i Press, 1974.

Kirch, Patrick Vinton. *Feathered Gods and Fishhooks.* Honolulu: University of Hawai'i Press, 1997.

Kirsten, Sven A. *The Book of Tiki: The Cult of Polynesian Pop in Fifties America.* Kōln: Taschen, 2000.

Pfouts, Chris. *Hula Girls and Tiki Gods.* Schiffer, PA: 2001.

Valerio, Valeri (translated by Paula Wissing). *Kingship and Sacrifice Ritual and Society in Ancient Hawaii.* Chicago: University of Chicago Press, 1985.

For More Information

For a primer on the Hawaiian kapu system, religion and heiau:
http://www.cr.nps.gov/history/online_books/kona/history1h.htm

For a primer on modern American tiki art:
http://www.shootinggallerysf.com/PastShows/2004/Sep_2004/
TikiShow2004.htm

ABOUT THE AUTHOR

Sophia V. Schweitzer, an award-winning freelance writer, has authored and co-authored numerous books, and has contributed to dozens of national publications. She specializes in Hawai'i-related subjects, nutrition, complementary medicine, and sustainable living. Her book *Kohala 'Āina, A History of North Kohala* (Mutual Publishing, November 2003) received a literary arts *Kahili* and the *Best-of-Show* in the annual statewide *Keep it Hawai'i* awards in 2004. Schweitzer lives in North Kohala on the Big Island with her husband and two poi dogs.

Costarring with Julie Andrews in the 1966 movie *Hawaii* based on James Michener's bestseller, Elizabeth Logue plays Noelani and Manu Tupou Keoki. The classic was released as a DVD in April 2005.

PHOTO CREDITS